SIMPLE PLEASURES MANDALA COLORING BOOK

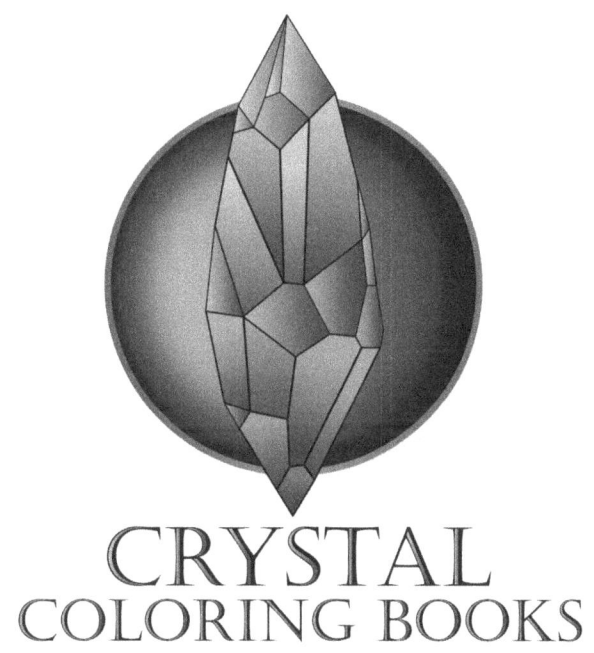

CRYSTAL COLORING BOOKS

Copyright © 2018 Crystal Coloring Books
All rights reserved.

ISBN: 9781731081766

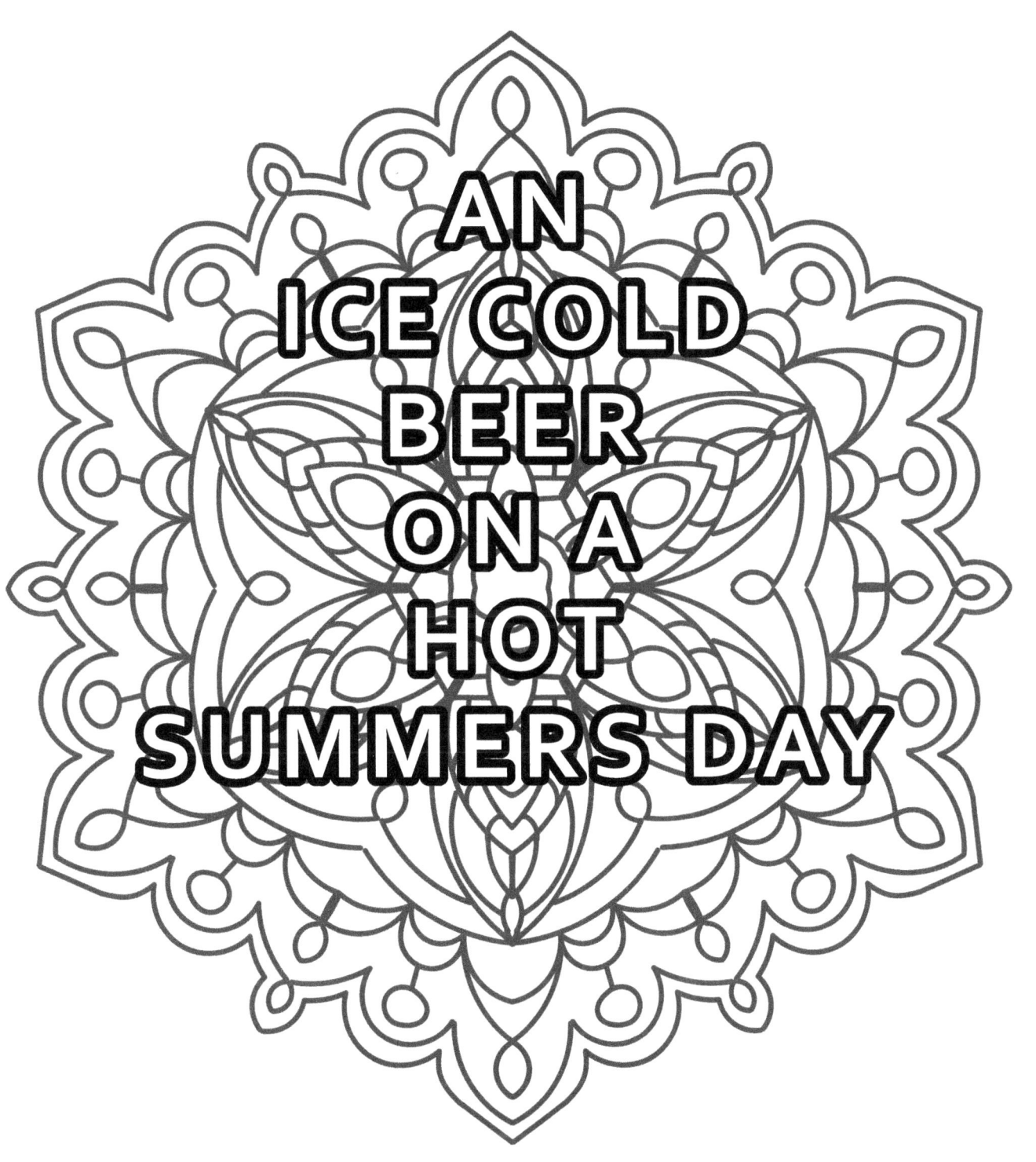

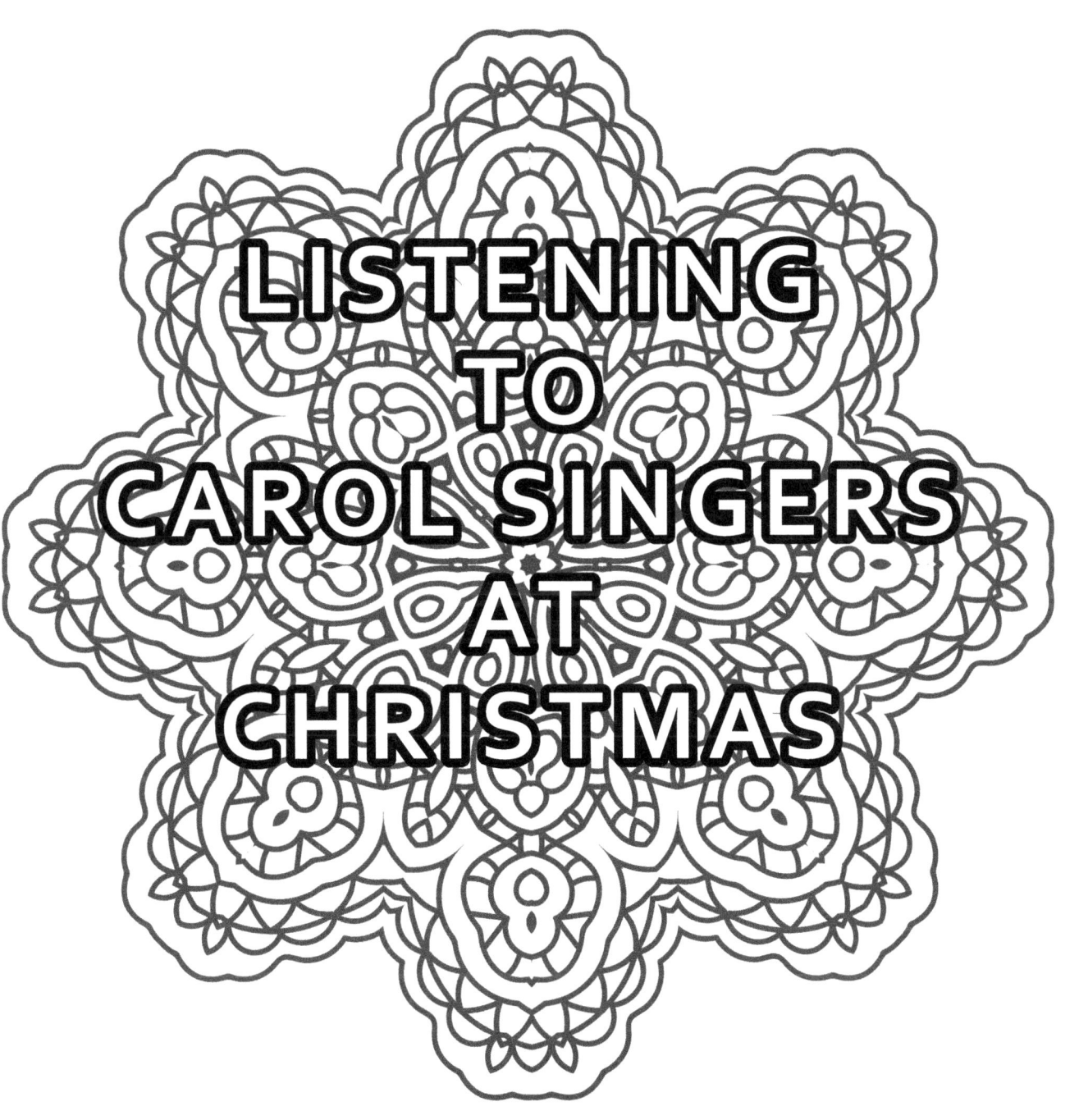

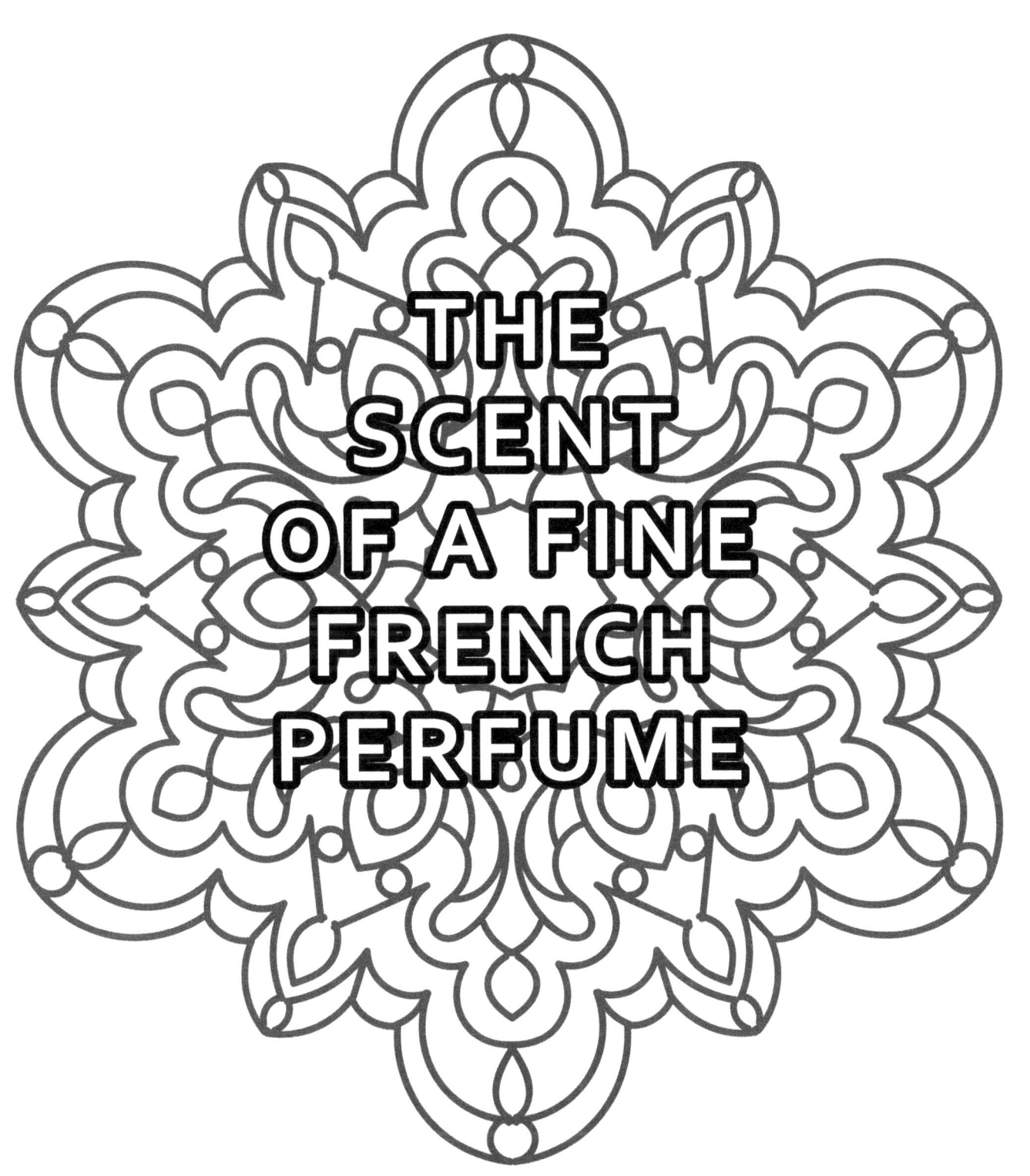

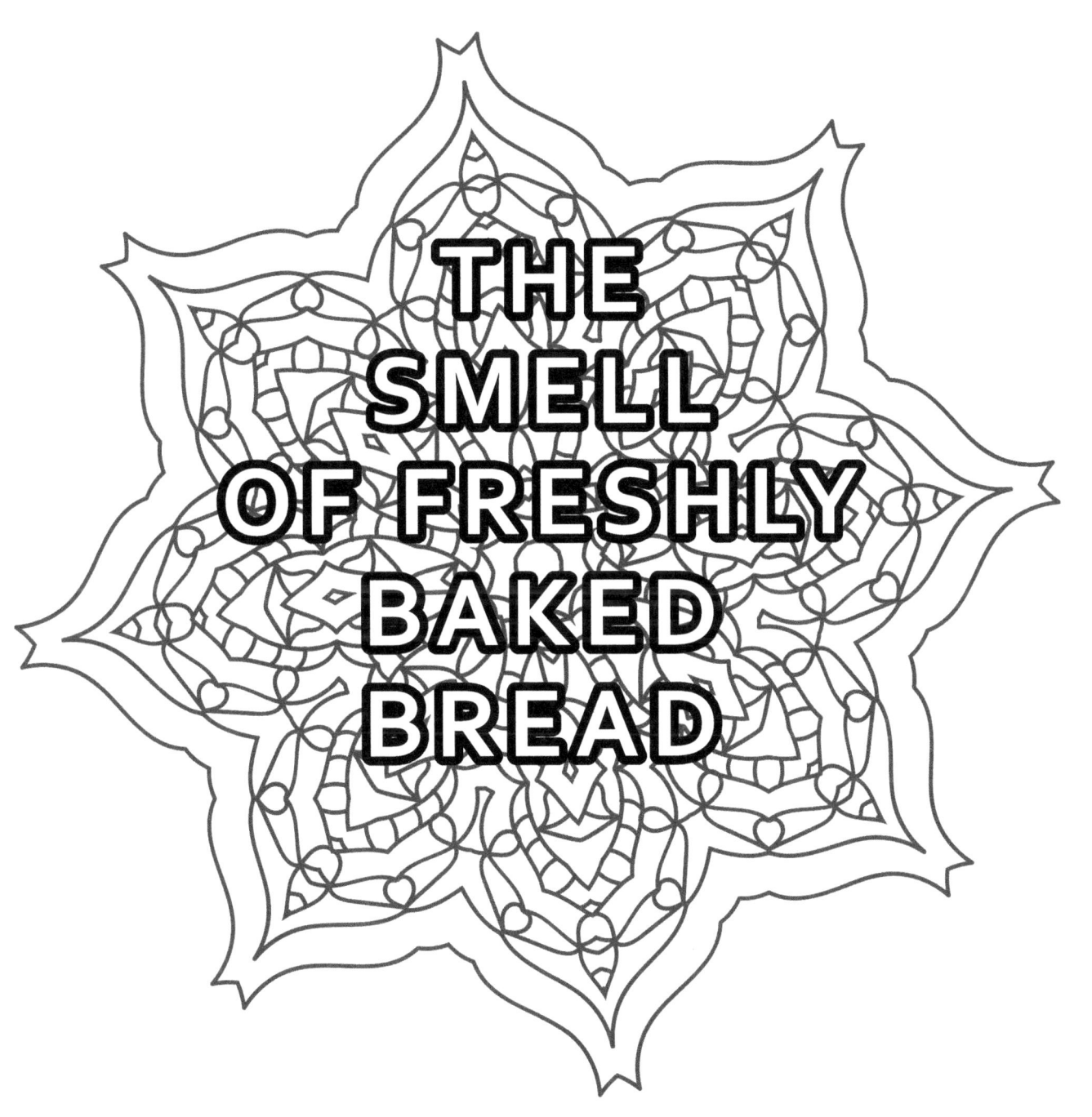

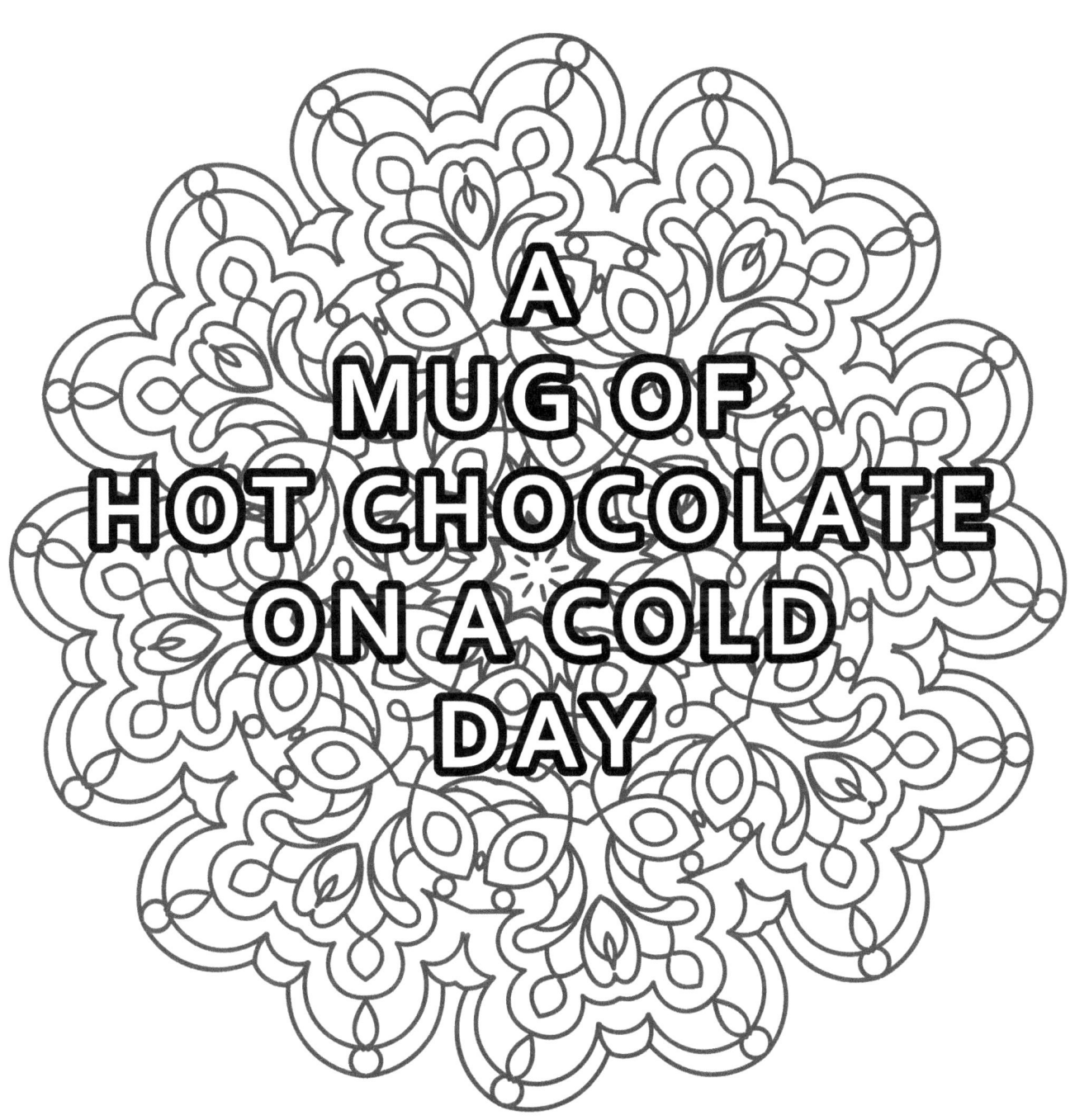

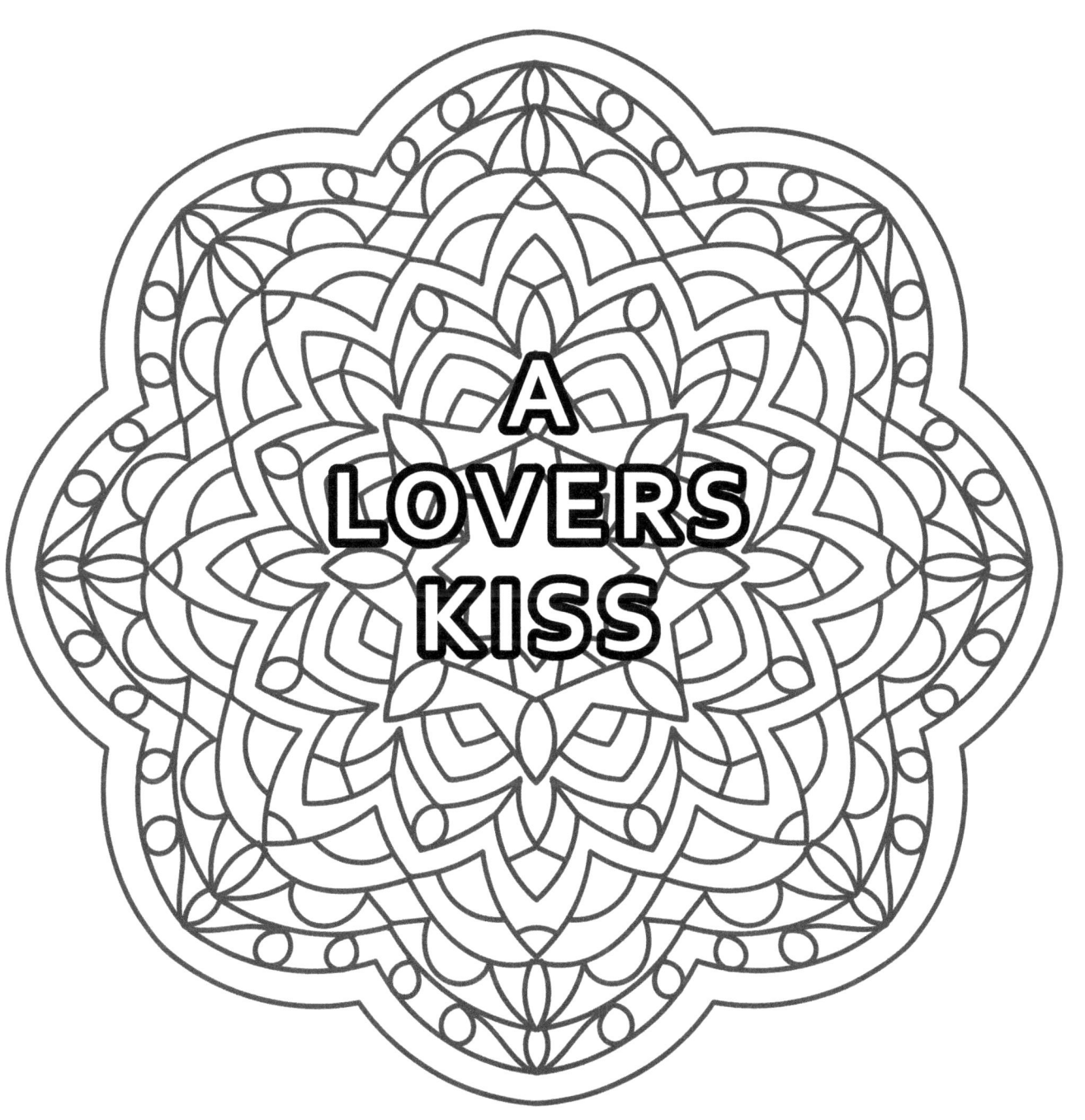

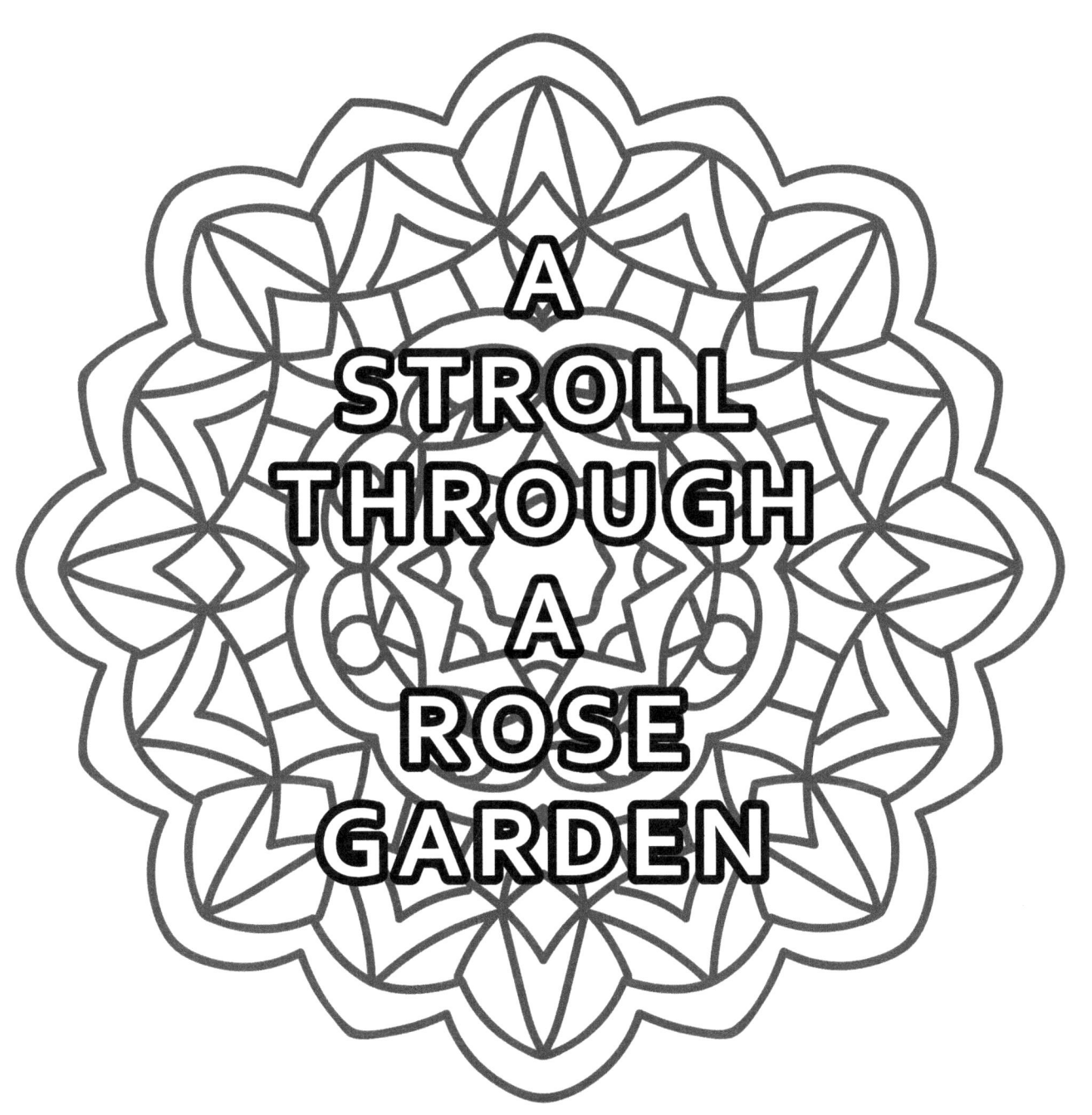

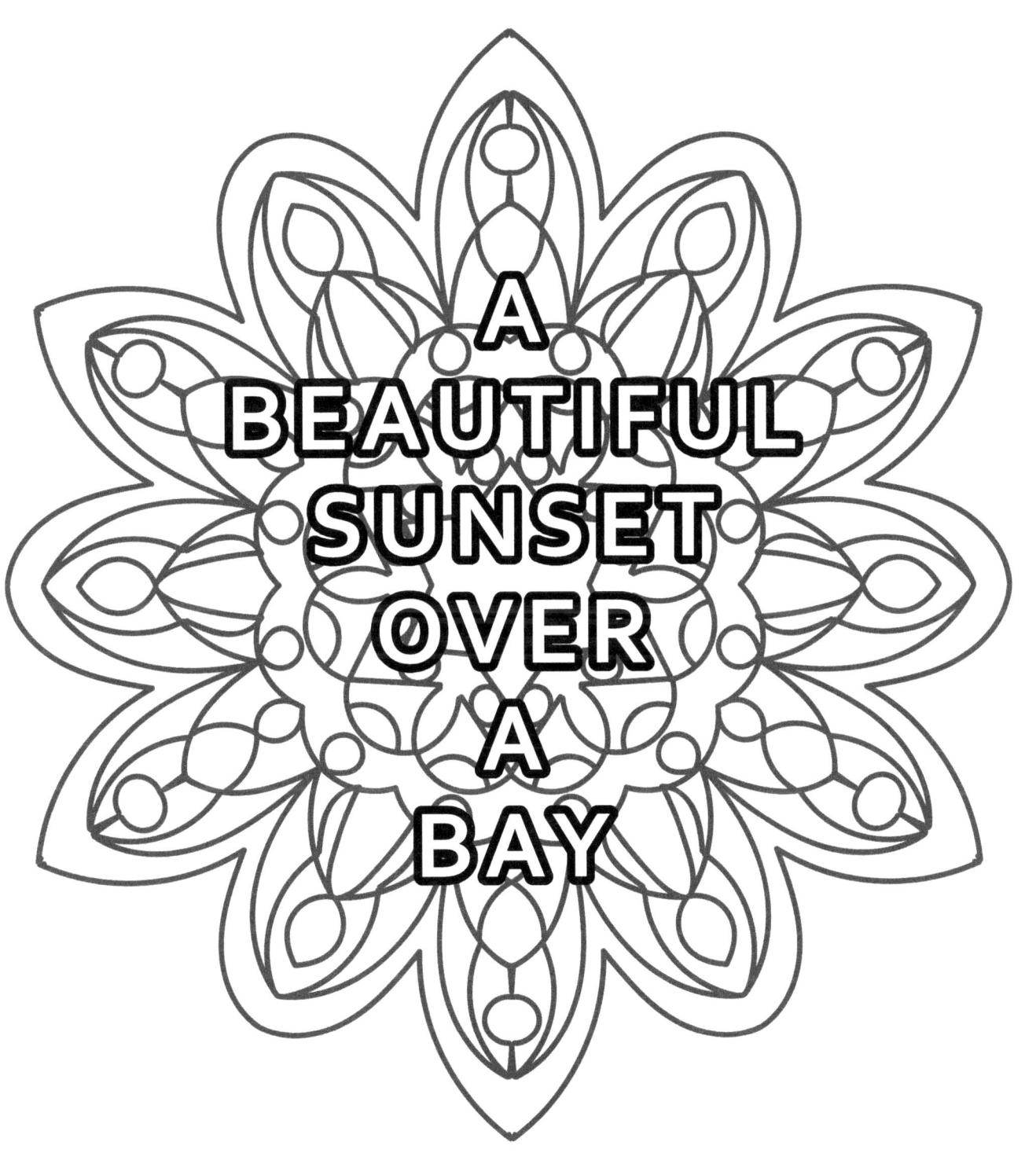

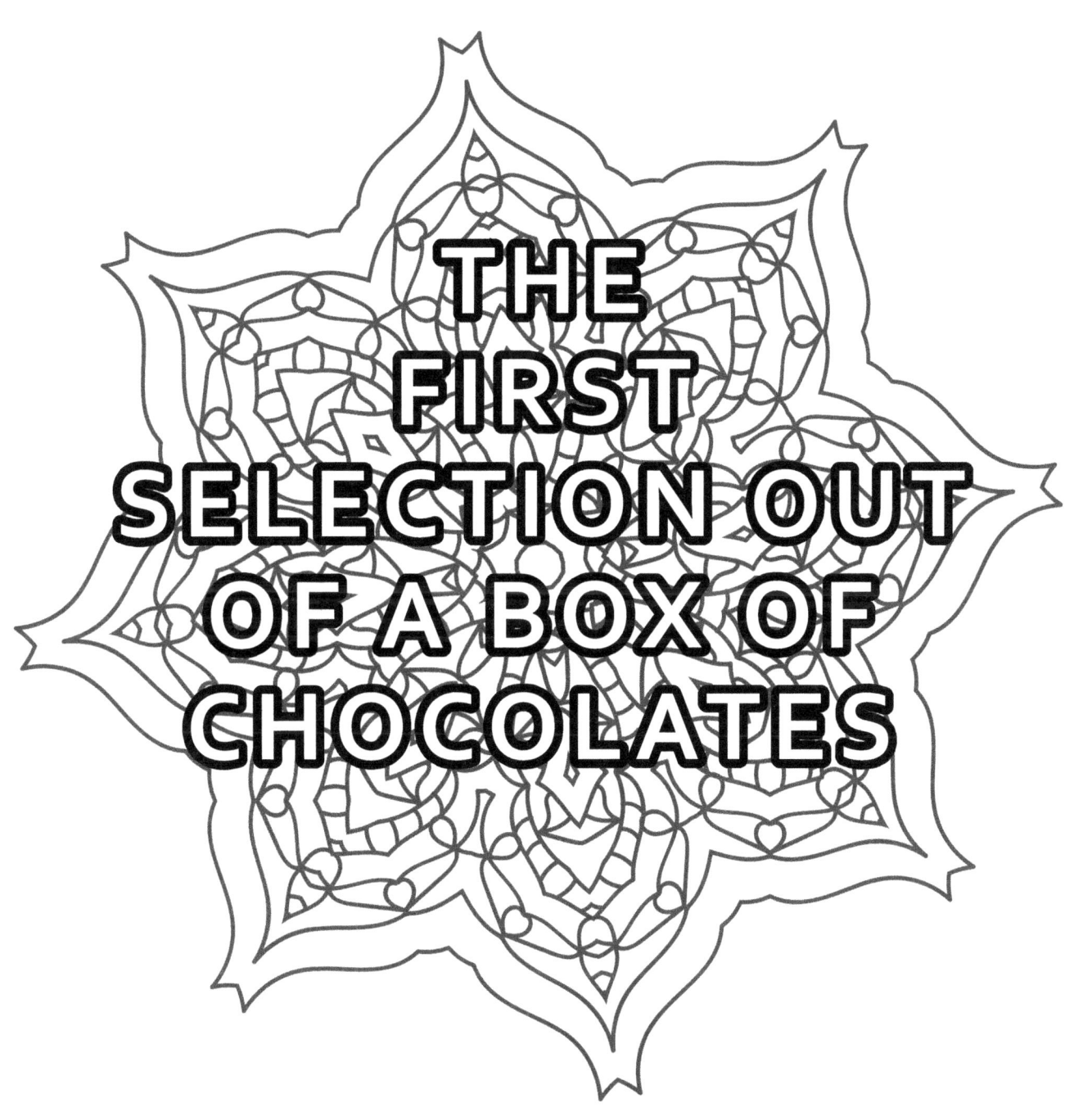

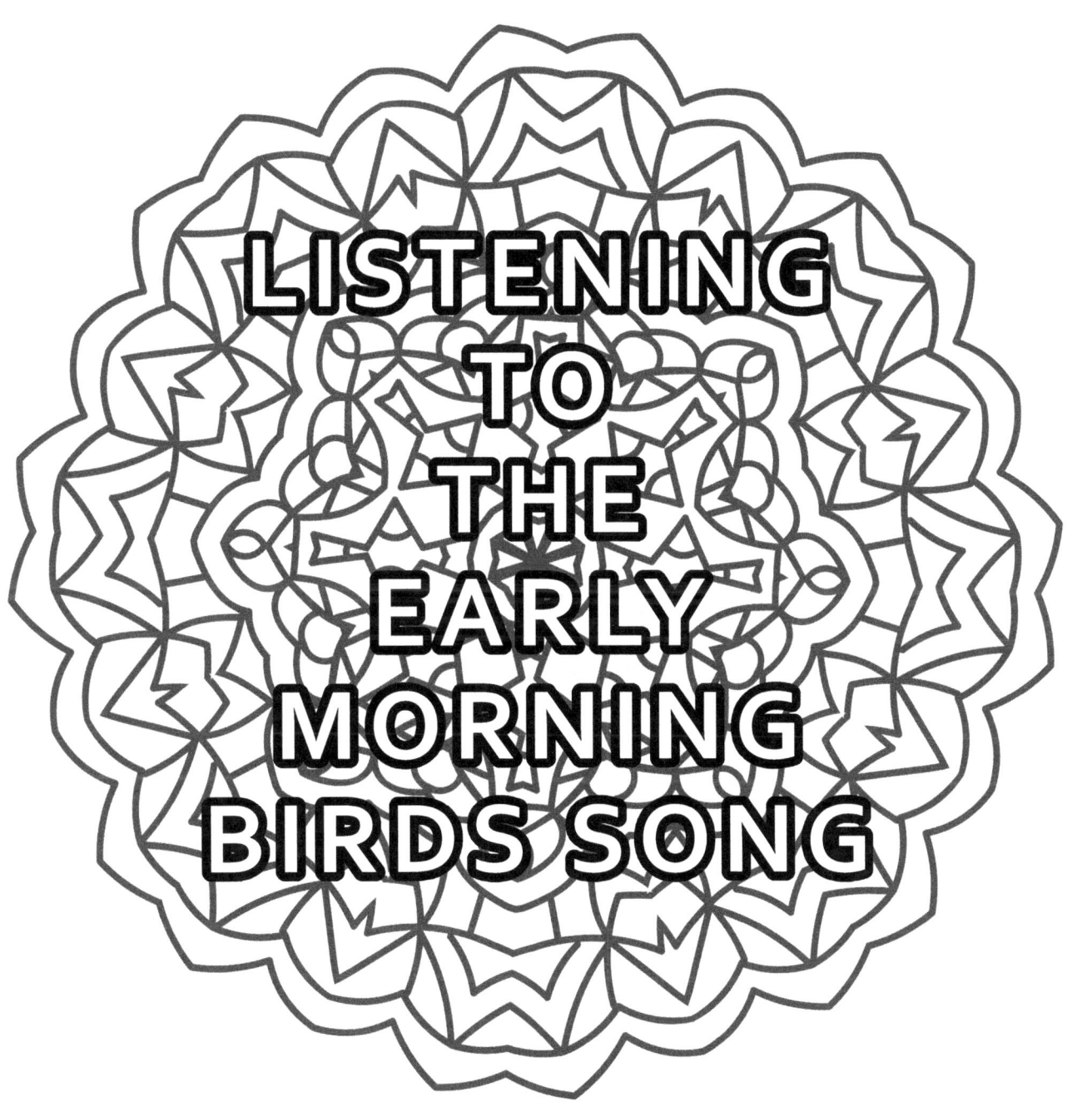

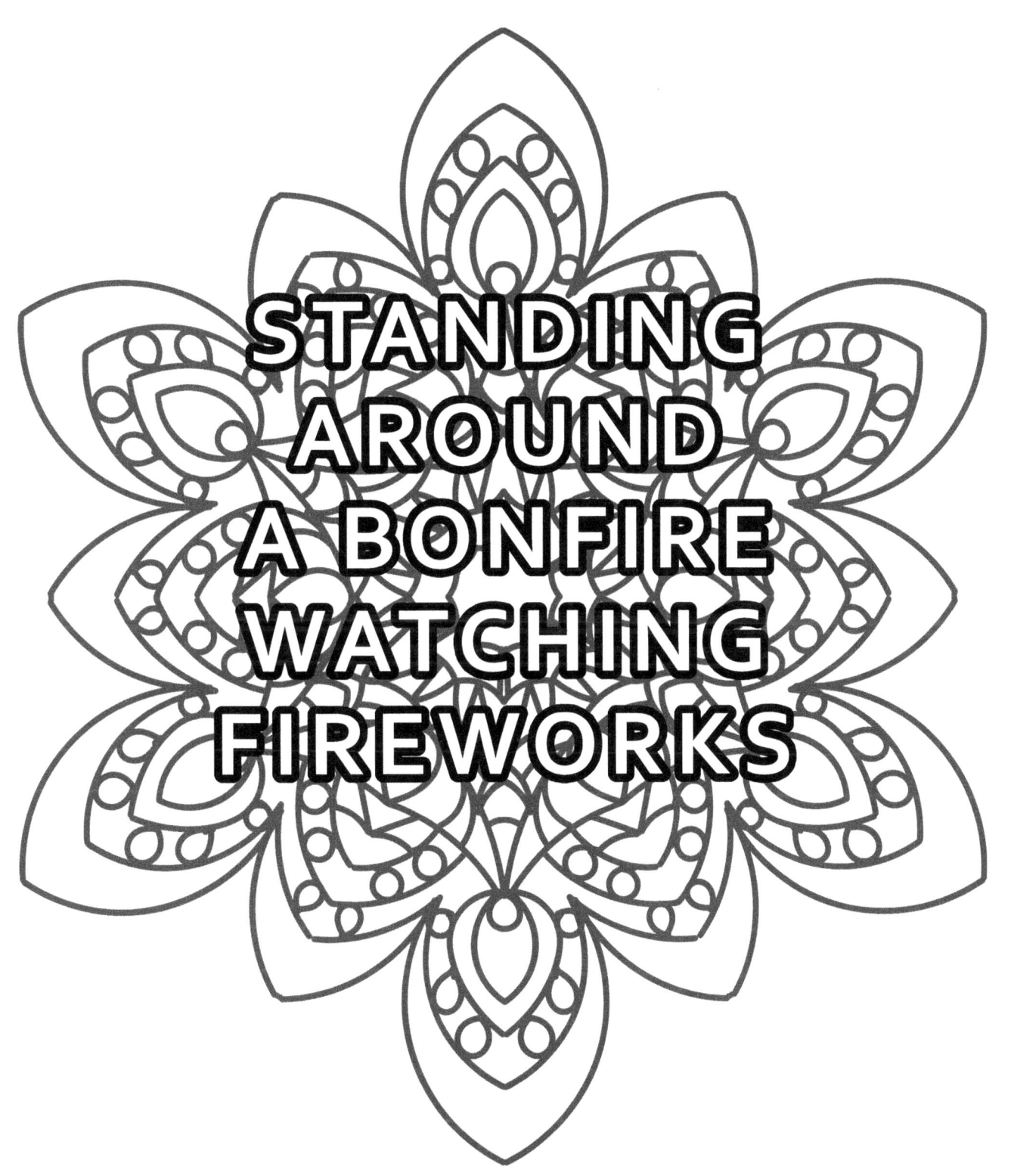

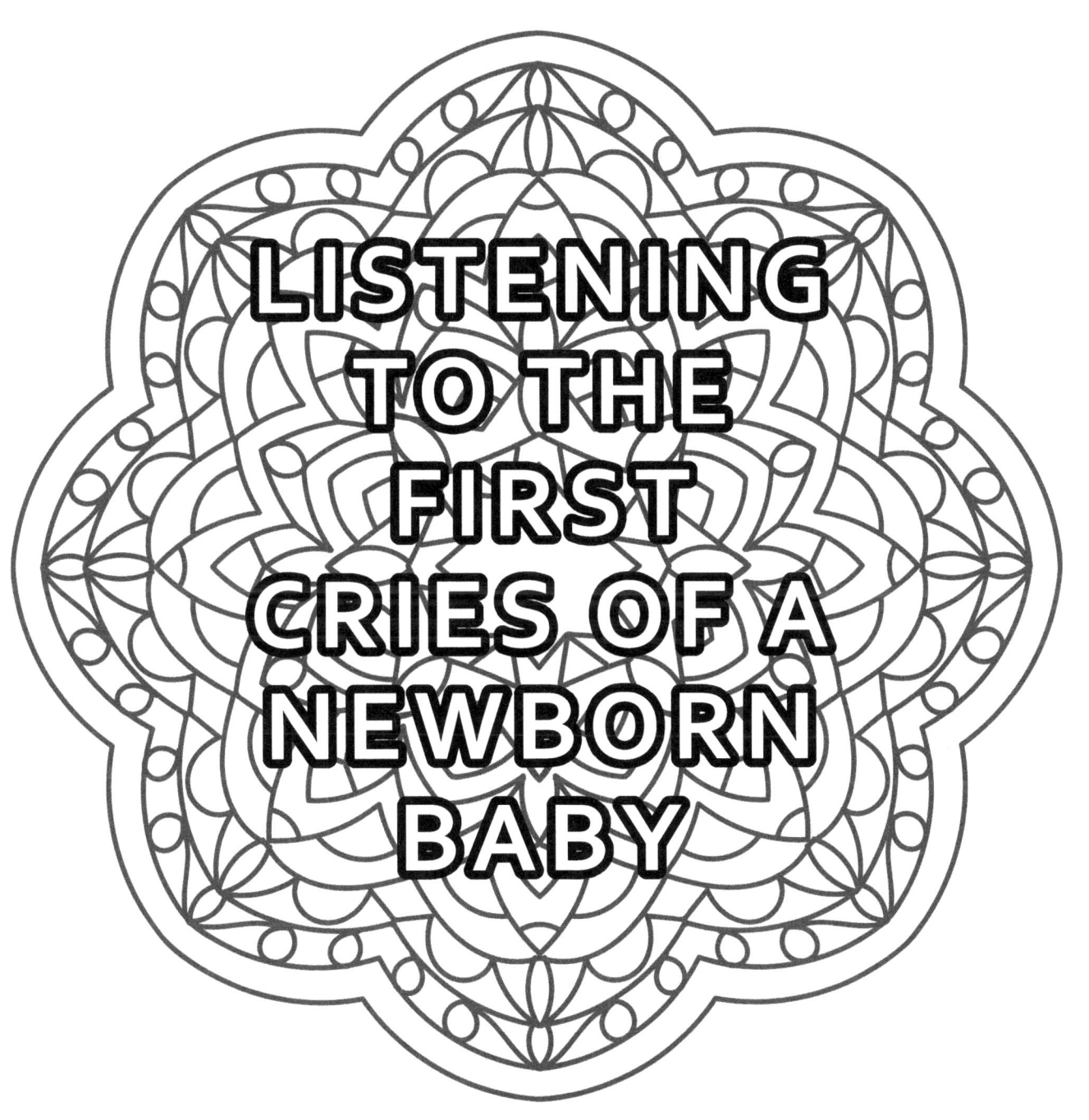

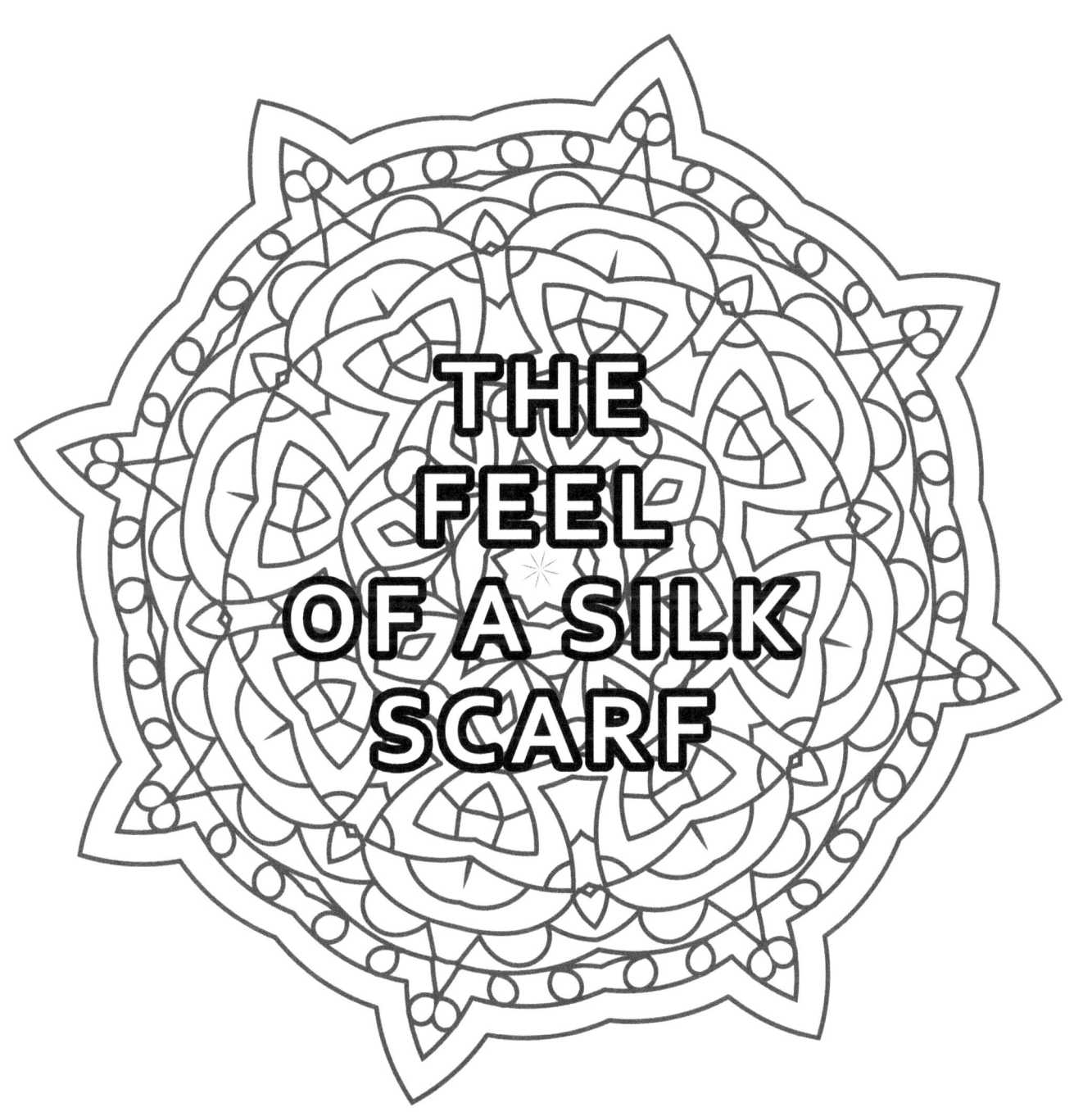

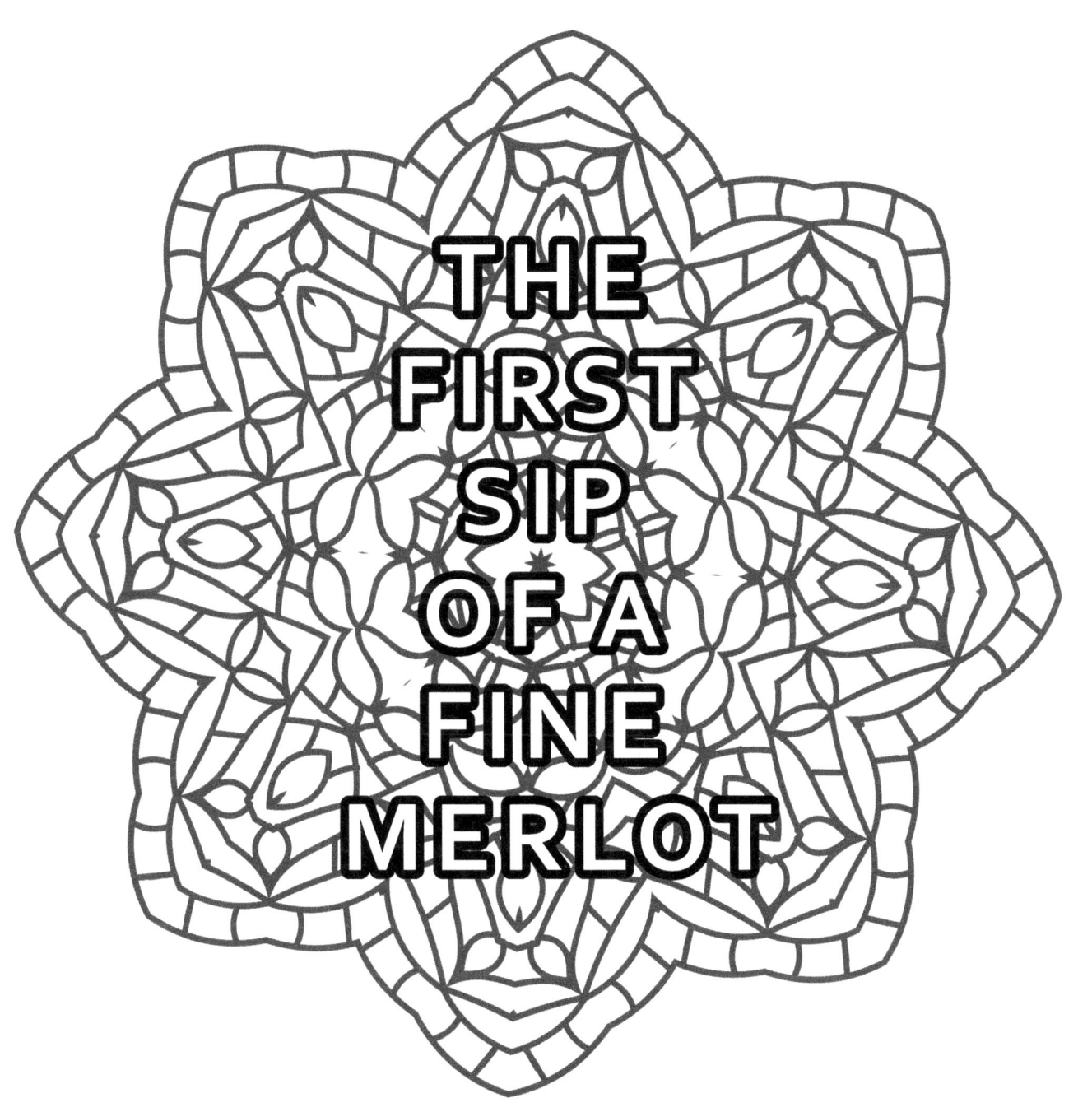

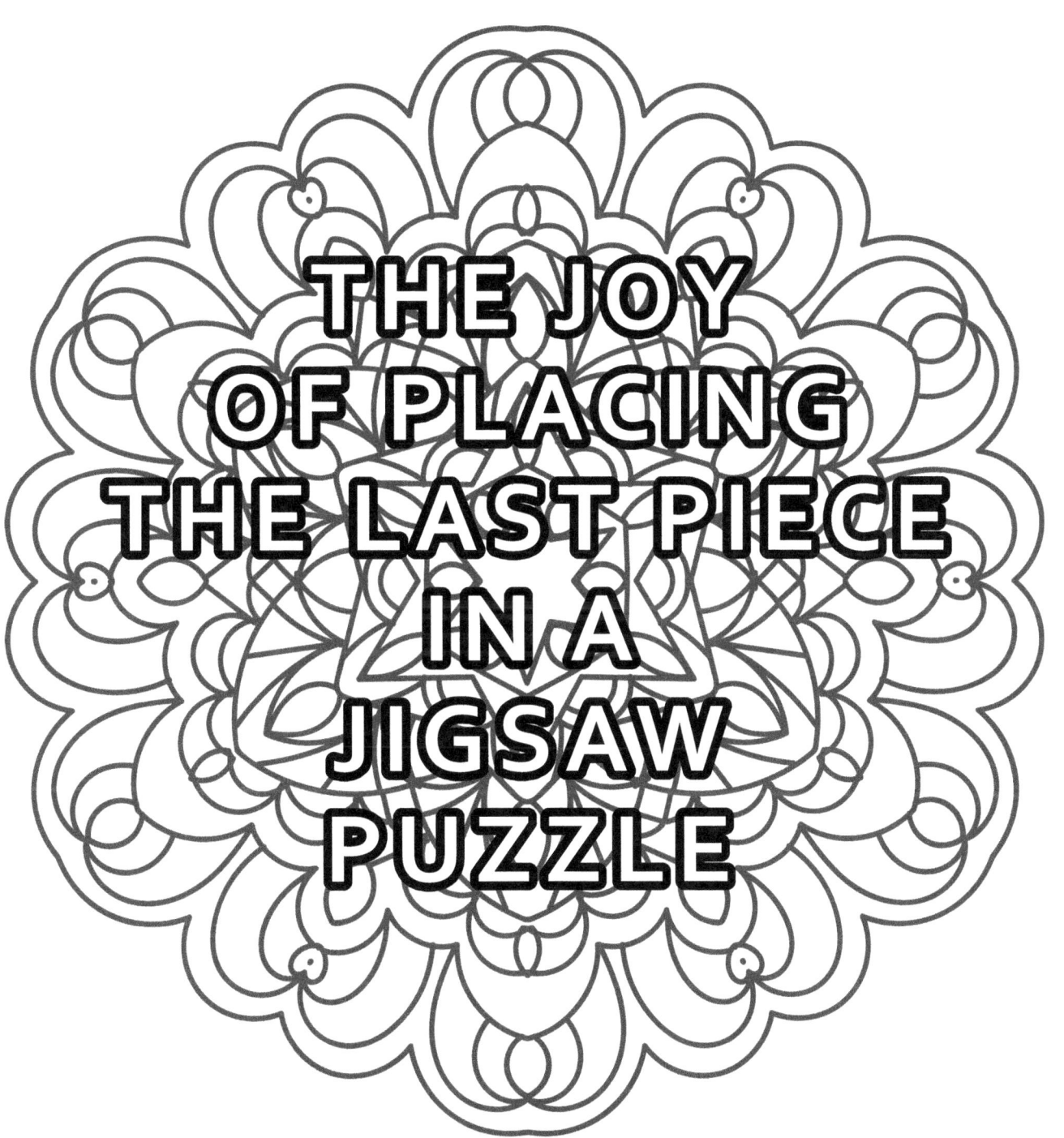

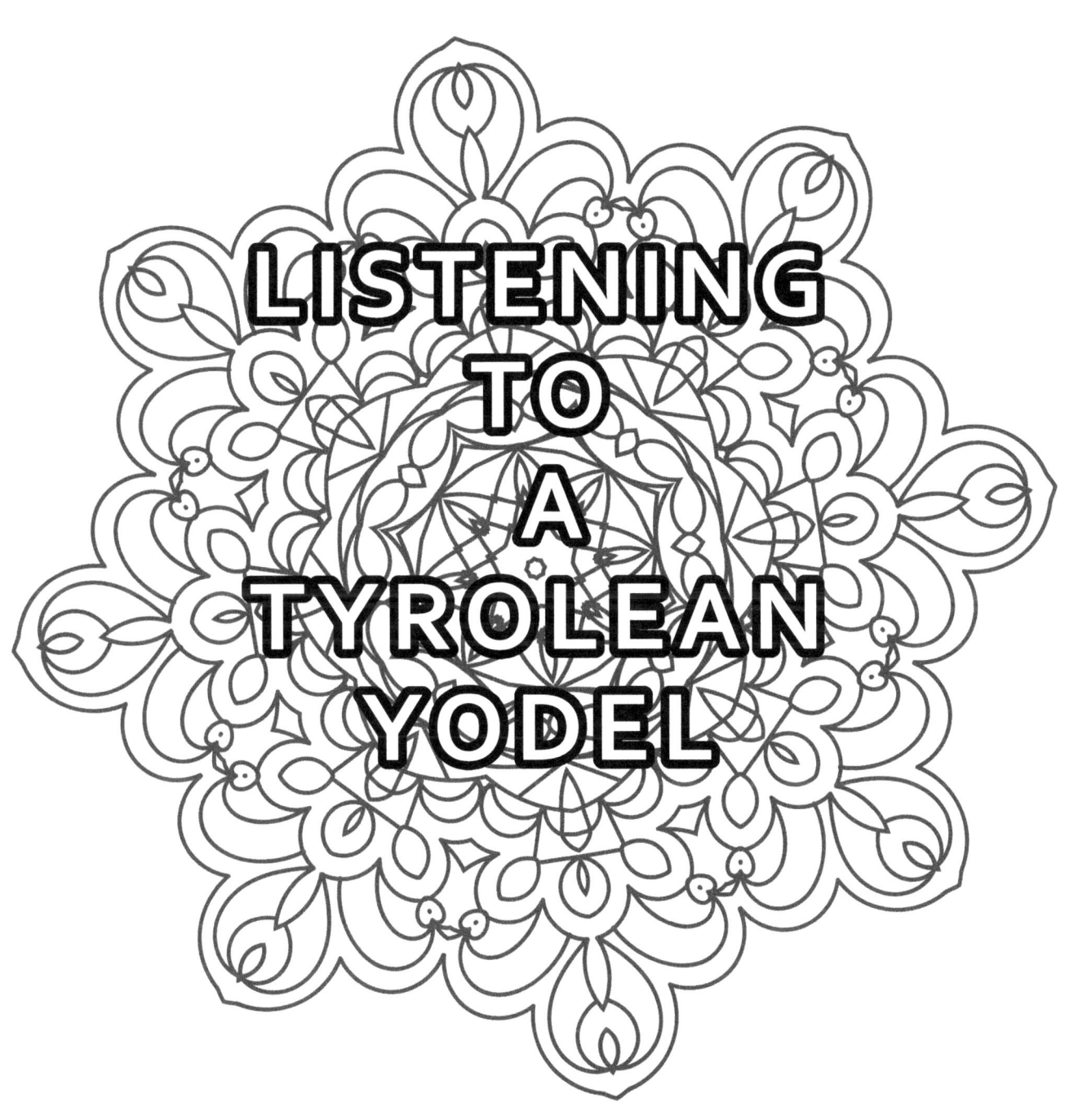

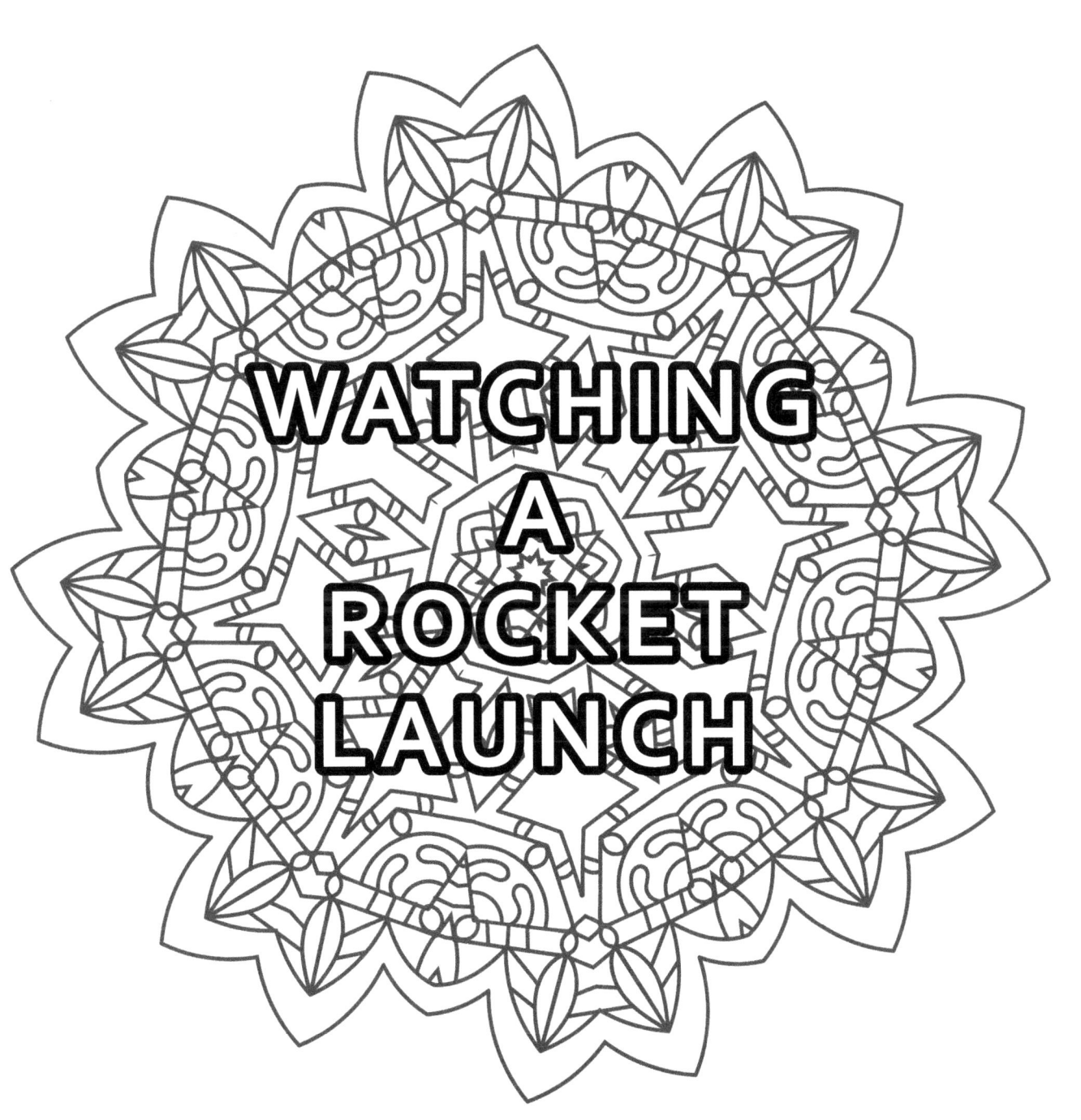

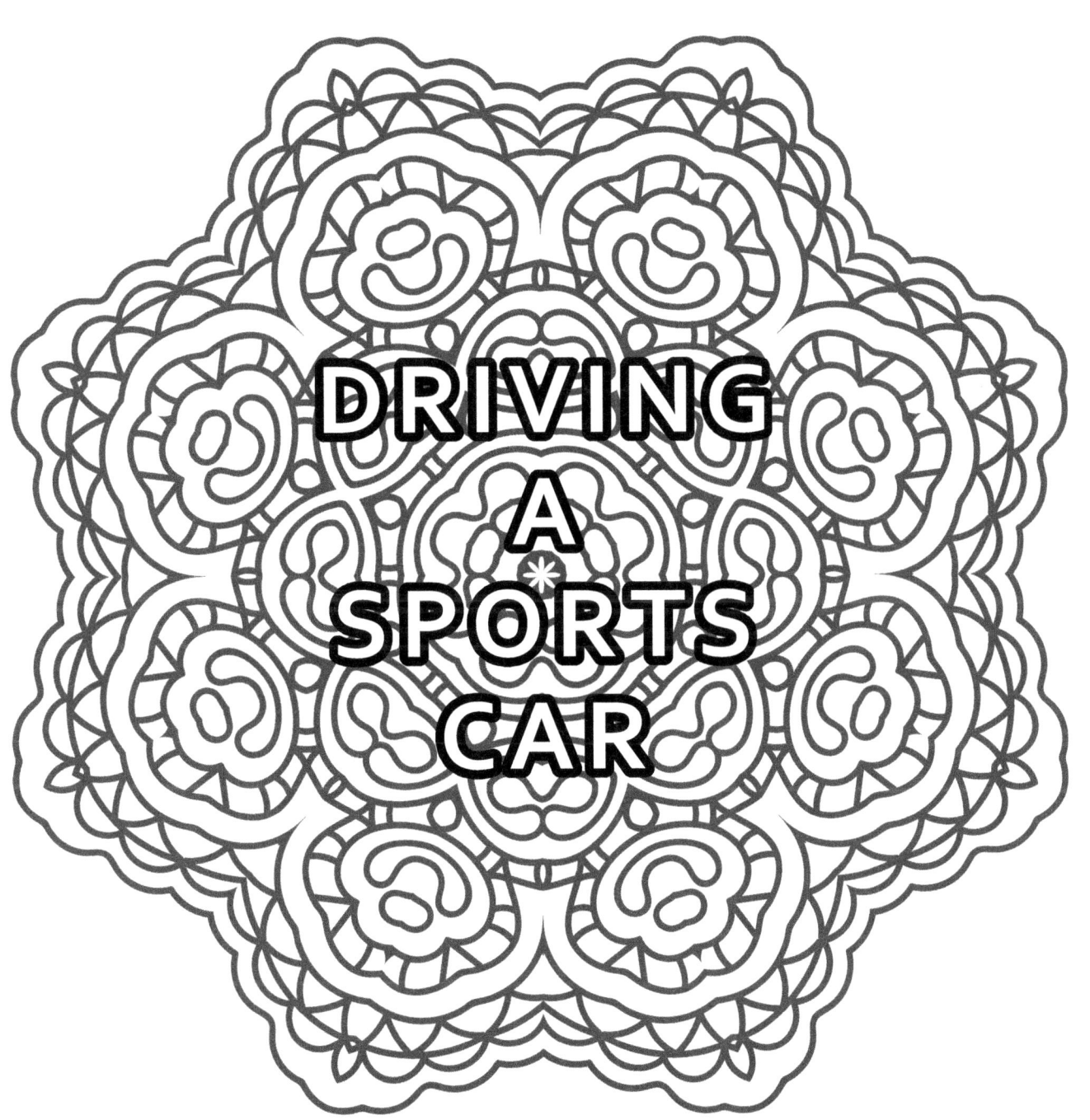

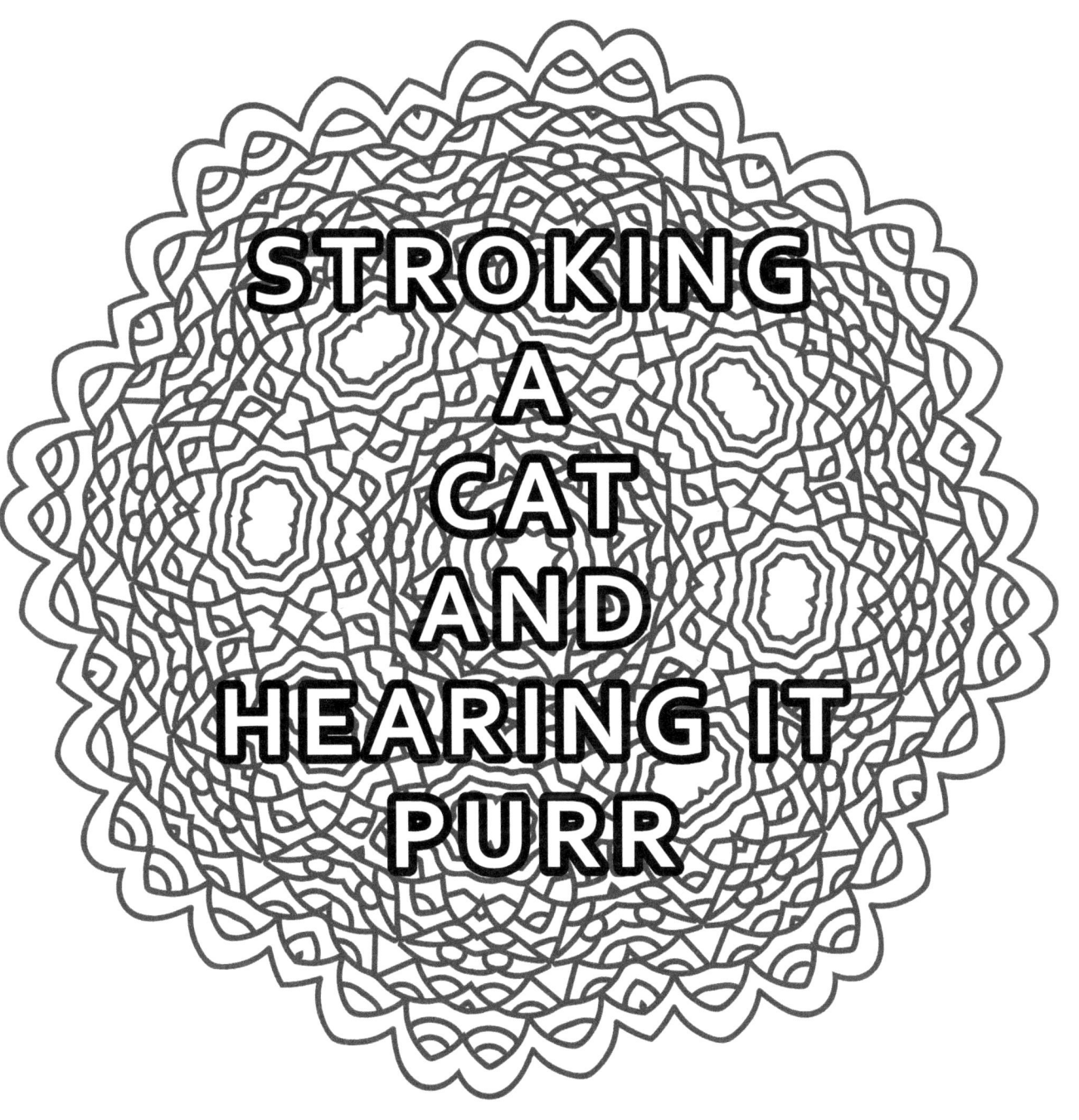

COLOR TEST PAGE

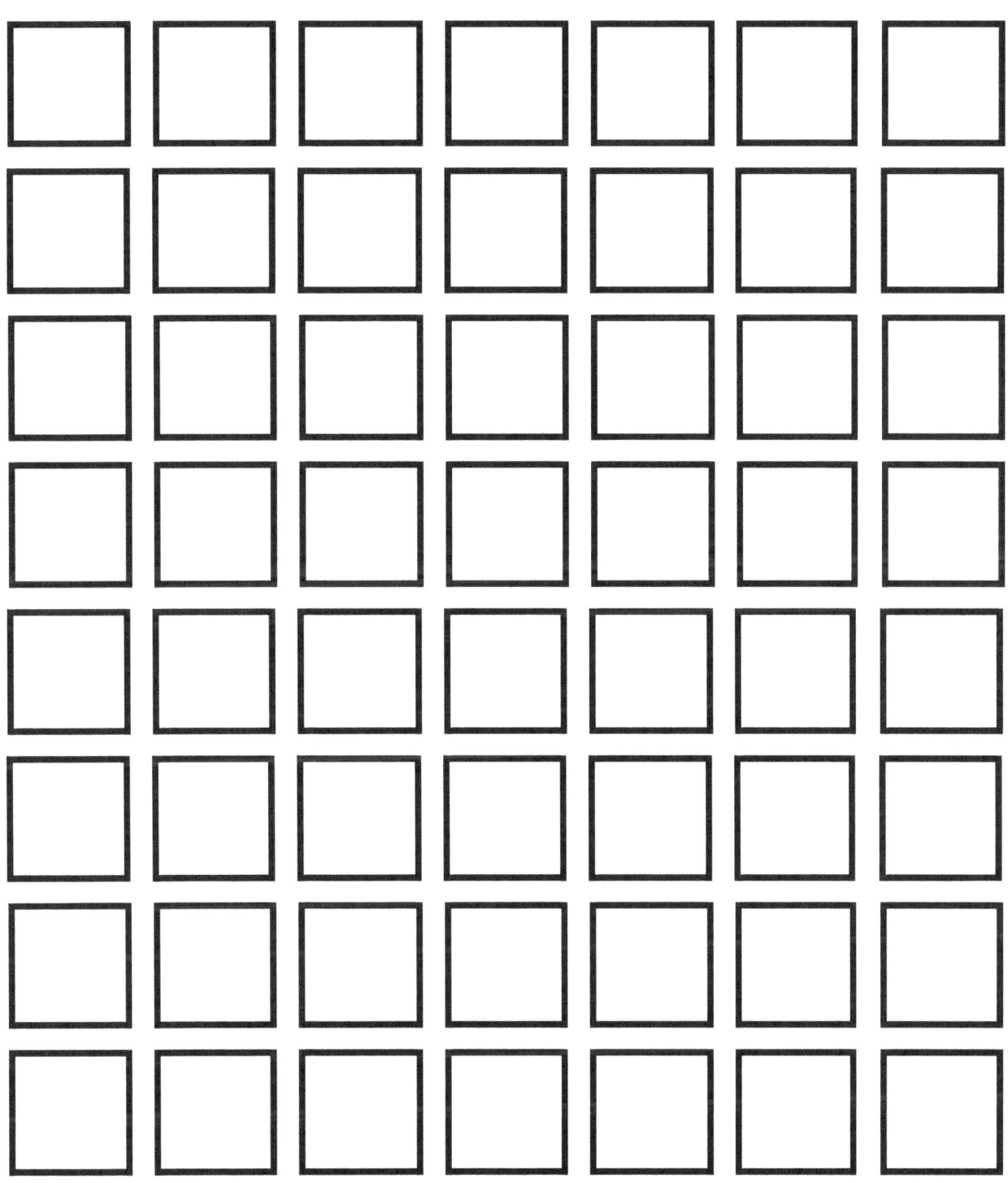

www.ingramcontent.com/pod-product-compliance
Lightning Source LLC
Chambersburg PA
CBHW082257220526
45469CB00009B/3047